COOKING
THE
WEST AFRICAN
WAY

First published in the United Kingdom in 2010 by
Lerner Books,
Dalton House,
60 Windsor Avenue,
London SW19 2RR

Website address: www.lernerbooks.co.uk

This edition was updated and edited for UK publication by Discovery Books Ltd., First Floor, 2 College Street, Ludlow, Shropshire SY8 1AN

British Library Cataloguing in Publication Data

Montgomery, Bertha Vining
Cooking the West African way. - New ed. - (Cooking around the world)
1. Cookery, West African - Juvenile literature
I. Title II. Nabwire, Constance R.
641.5'966

ISBN-13: 978 0 7613 4396 7

Printed in China

cooking around the world

COOKING
THE
WEST AFRICAN
WAY

Bertha Vining Montgomery and Constance Nabwire

Lerner

Lerner Books • London • New York • Minneapolis

Contents

Introduction

West African men and women dressed in brightly coloured clothing crowd the marketplace in the coastal city of Lagos, Nigeria. They laugh with friends and barter for fresh fruit and vegetables. Here, cooks use whatever foods are in season, adding chillies and other spices to give dishes a kick. Fufu, peanut stew and jollof rice – foods that are often thought of as typically African – come from West Africa.

The ingredients in spinach stew (recipe on page 57) are easy to find. The dish is also high in nutrition and takes very little time to prepare.

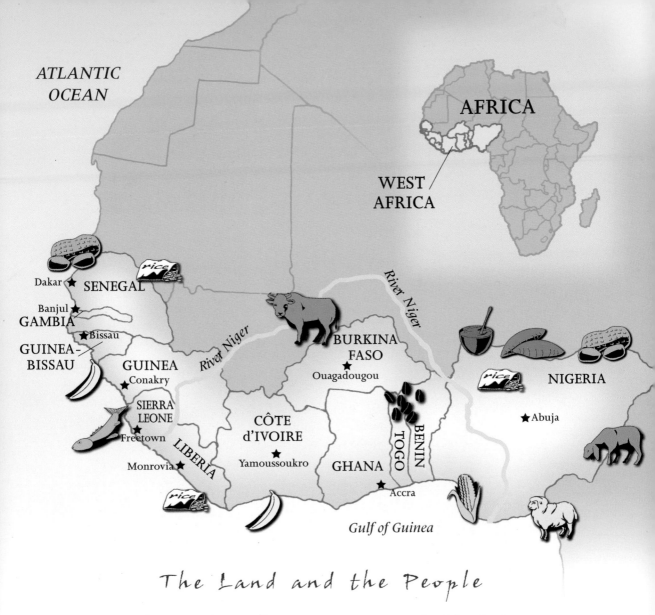

ATLANTIC OCEAN

AFRICA

WEST AFRICA

Dakar ★ SENEGAL

Banjul ★
GAMBIA

★Bissau

GUINEA-BISSAU

GUINEA
Conakry ●

SIERRA LEONE
Freetown ★

Monrovia ★ LIBERIA

River Niger

BURKINA FASO
Ouagadougou ●

River Niger

CÔTE d'IVOIRE

Yamoussoukro ★

GHANA

TOGO

BENIN

Accra ●

NIGERIA

★Abuja

Gulf of Guinea

The Land and the People

West Africa is a cluster of countries jutting into the Atlantic Ocean. The region's major nations include Nigeria, Senegal, Ghana and Côte d'Ivoire. The land is low and flat. Some of it is covered with forests, while other parts are made up of grassy plains called savannahs. A region on the coasts is hot, humid and rainy all year long. The rest of West Africa is also hot throughout the year, with both a wet and a dry season.

People of many different ethnic and religious backgrounds live in West Africa. Although most West Africans are black, they are further divided into hundreds of ethnic groups, each with its own language and traditions. Islam is the dominant religion in the region, but West Africans also practise Christianity. Many West Africans practise a traditional religion in addition to either Islam or Christianity.

The lives of West Africans also vary greatly, depending on whether they live in the city or the country. Rural dwellers have lives that are very much the same as those of their ancestors. They usually live in villages with other people of the same ethnic group. While some villages have houses made of modern materials such as cement and metal, many people still live in houses made of clay or dried mud, with roofs of grass or palm leaves.

The people of a West African village depend on each other like members of an extended family. In fact, it is not unusual for everyone in a village to be related in some way. Traditionally, the men are responsible for farming the land that surrounds the village. The women help with the farming work and also cook and take care of the children. Even the children have their role in the life of the village. They help the adults wherever they can, until they are old enough to take on adult responsibilities.

Many villages don't have modern machines or tools for cooking or farming. Ploughing is often done with a wooden plough pulled by oxen. Food is prepared with the same kinds of hand tools that have been used in Africa for hundreds of years.

One traditional cooking tool found in nearly every West African home is the pestle and mortar. A pestle is a club-shaped utensil that is used with a mortar, a sturdy bowl, to grind or pound foods. Another essential tool is the sieve, a square or round utensil with a fine wire mesh across the bottom. It is used to remove small particles from larger pieces of food. The most important tool used in traditional African cooking is fire. While ovens are used in the cities, where gas and electricity are available, most rural West Africans still cook over a fire, just as their ancestors did.

The Food

Because food is sometimes scarce in certain parts of Africa, West African cooks have learned to work with whatever they have. The dishes are versatile enough that, if an ingredient is not available, it is always possible to substitute it with another or leave it out.

The main meal, which is usually served in the afternoon or evening, is likely to be made up of a thick stew or soup and a starchy food. The stew or soup usually contains a variety of vegetables and perhaps a little meat, poultry or fish. The starch can be anything from bread to rice to fufu – a food that tastes a bit like mashed potatoes. In West Africa, the stew and the starch are often combined to make a one-pot meal, such as jollof rice.

Young Ghanaians enjoy a bowl of fufu (recipe on page 32) and fish. Using their right hands, the children use the fufu to scoop up the fish.

Most people in West Africa follow the Islamic faith. Muslims (followers of Islam) pray five times each day, facing towards Mecca. This city in Saudi Arabia is the birthplace of Muhammad, the founder of Islam.

West Africans may only eat two meals per day, but they often enjoy a snack. Typical snacks include be roasted plantains or meat on a skewer. In cities, these and other snack foods are sold on the street.

Because very few people have a fridge, the cooking of West Africa is based on fresh foods. In the villages, people grow all of their own fruit and vegetables in small gardens. Although the people who live in the cities may have fridges and rely somewhat on tinned foods, they are still likely to visit the market every day to buy fresh fruit and vegetables.

West African farmers grow cacao beans, yams, peanuts, sweetcorn, plantains and cassavas. It is hard to believe that the vast majority of these plants were introduced to Africa by the Europeans and Arabs. Some of the few plants used for food that are native to West Africa are oil palm, millet and sorghum.

Fish are abundant along the West African coast. Chicken and beef are not so plentiful. One reason that soups and stews are such staples in West Africa is that they can make a little meat stretch to feed many people. It is not unusual for a meal to contain no meat at all. On the coasts or near large lakes, fish is cheaper than meat and people often combine meat and fish in the same dish. Chicken is usually saved for guests or special occasions. Meat, poultry and fish, like fruit and vegetables, are usually served fresh, although they are sometimes preserved by smoking or drying.

To this day, most West African cooks do not use recipes when cooking. In fact, until recently it was considered a disgrace in some areas of West Africa to write down recipes. Instead, they were passed down from generation to generation by memory.

West Africa is thought of as one of the most traditionally African regions on the continent, but European and Indian dishes have crept into the cuisine. Foods from Britain and France caught on when the two countries governed the nations of West Africa. The nations gained independence one by one in the mid-1950s and early 1960s. Britain, which ruled India for decades, also introduced Indian foods to West Africa. Since then, curry has become popular in the region.

The recipes in this book were collected from women in different countries all over West Africa and then adapted. A few of the recipes have been changed slightly to suit Western tastes. For example, fufu is traditionally made with pounded yams or plantains and some recipes would contain less meat if they were being prepared in West Africa. Also, many traditional West African foods are spicy hot, often because fiery chillies are among the ingredients. The recipes included in this book are spicy, but not as spicy as they would be if prepared in West Africa. Everyone has different tastes. You need to be aware of this as you are cooking and adjust the seasonings accordingly. For the most part, however, the recipes are authentic. Once you have had a taste of West African cooking, you might try varying the meats and vegetables, to make up your own combinations.

At an outdoor market, a seller carries fresh yams, as well as her baby, to her market stall. Yams are a staple of West African cooking and are the inspiration for some of the region's most popular festivals.

Festivals

West Africa hosts a variety of festivals throughout the year. Traditional foods play an important part in each celebration. In fact, a number of these events are all about food – they may honour a local harvest or celebrate the end of a famine.

West Africans celebrate the harvest of yams more than any other crop. For the Ewe people in Ghana, the September yam harvest marks the beginning of their new year. The Ewe people dance, drum, wear animal masks and display fetishes – small stone carvings of animals that are believed to protect their owners. In the evening, the people turn off all of the lights. Town leaders called fetish priests lead a procession through the streets. The priests carry a bundle of rope and leaves, believed to cleanse the town of evil.

At the end of the procession, the priests bury the bundle and pray that no evil crosses over it. When the sun rises, the farmers parade around the town to mark the new yam harvest. The people eat a feast of the many foods made from yams.

Nigerians celebrate the Iri-Ji festival. In Nigeria, ji means 'yam', and yams are believed to represent life. The celebration provides a link between the living and their ancestors. Traditional tribal dances and music entertain the revellers while they feast on *futari*, a dish made from yams and squash. Cooks also pound yams to make fufu.

For two days in February, the people of Sokoto, Nigeria, hold the Argungu fishing festival. Thousands of men and boys wade into the Sokoto River carrying nets stretched over bamboo poles. Although it is the only time during the year that fishing is allowed in the

river, participants are only allowed 45 minutes to fish. Some catch fish that weigh as much as 65 kilograms. After watching the men fish, villagers listen to music, watch traditional dances and cheer for the boys, who compete in wrestling matches. The festival includes foods made with the fish that are caught.

In the Ghanaian countryside, the Ga people hold the Homowo festival each August. *Homowo* means 'hooting at hunger'. Long ago, this region suffered a severe famine. Ever since, the Ga people have held the festival to give thanks for good harvests. The Ga people eat milled corn and fish in memory of their ancestors. To the beat of drums, cooks pour cornmeal and palm oil around the houses in the town to protect those who live there from hunger.

During the Argungu festival in Nigeria, men and boys fish against the clock in the Sokoto River. The participants use the nets to make the fish swim into shallow water, where they are scooped up. The gourds help to keep the nets above the water.

Other West African celebrations honour religious festivals or long-standing traditions. The most important Islamic festival is Eid ul-Fitr, the big feast that brings Ramadan fasting to an end. Ramadan celebrates the ninth month in the Islamic calendar – the holiest month of the year in Islamic belief. Muslims fast from sunrise to sunset to honour the festival. To West Africans in Nigeria, Senegal and Guinea, Eid ul-Fitr is the most important day of the year. In Nigeria, Muslim men begin the day by praying at a mosque (an Islamic house of worship). In the afternoon, each city holds a festival featuring a parade that ends at the palace of the local ruler, called the emir. Horsemen in uniform and people swinging swords and spears march to the beat of drums and the sound of blowing horns. Entertainers such as acrobats, jugglers and snake charmers delight crowds on the palace grounds. People enjoy salads and lamb roasted over a fire.

In Côte d'Ivoire, a country that was once a French colony, city dwellers speak French and follow French customs. Many people are Christians and go to church on Christmas Eve, enjoying a big dinner called *le réveillon* at midnight. *Le réveillon* means 'to wake up to a new day'. For dessert, celebrants eat Yule log cake, which decorates the centre of the table during the meal. In other West African countries, many of which were ruled by Britain, families may celebrate on Christmas day. Sometimes, traditional British holiday foods, such as Christmas pudding, are served, but many people eat West African foods, such as fufu and soups or stews, instead.

When a child is born to the Yoruba in south-western Nigeria, the family celebrates with a naming ceremony called Ikomo. Ikomo is believed to welcome the child into the community. A high priest, called the Baba Lawo, leads the ceremony. The child's aunt gathers honey, water and salt – foods that will be sprinkled on the baby's tongue. The honey represents hope for a sweet, good life for the child, water confirms wishes that the baby will be as mighty as the ocean, and salt serves as a reminder that life isn't always good. Once the baby has tasted the foods, guests dab a little of the mixture onto

Holding his prayer beads, a Nigerian looks out over the River Niger, which flows in a great arc until it empties into the Gulf of Guinea.

their tongues. Then the oldest family member announces the baby's name. The ceremony ends with a big feast that might include jollof rice, spicy kebabs, peanut stew and ginger-roasted fish.

Countries that were once European colonies, celebrate their day of independence. Each August, Senegal marks its independence from France in 1960. Senegalese National Day is one of the country's most popular holidays. Parades, music and good food put everybody in a festive mood. Senegalese families may dine on *yassa* – chicken marinated in chilli sauce and fried in a frying pan – a dish reserved for special occasions.

Before You Begin

Cooking any dish, plain or complicated, is easier and more fun if you are familiar with the ingredients. West African cooking makes use of some ingredients that you may not know. You should also be familiar with the special terms that will be used in various recipes in this book. Therefore, *before* you start cooking any of the dishes in this book, study the following 'dictionary' of cooking utensils, cooking terms and special ingredients. Review the Careful Cook section on page 20 and be sure to read through each recipe from beginning to end. Then you will be ready to shop for ingredients and organize the equipment that you will need. Once you have assembled everything, you can begin to cook.

Coconut crisps (recipe on page 39) surround a bowl of kulikuli (recipe on page 38), a snack that is made from ground peanuts.

The Careful Cook

Whenever you cook, there are certain safety rules you must always keep in mind. Even experienced cooks follow these rules when they are in the kitchen.

- Always wash your hands before handling food. Thoroughly wash raw vegetables and fruits to remove dirt and chemicals. Wash uncooked poultry, fish and meat under cold water.
- Use a chopping board when cutting up vegetables and fruit. Be sure to cut carefully.
- Long hair or loose clothing can easily catch fire if brought near the hobs of a cooker. If you have long hair, tie it back.
- Turn all pan handles towards the back of the cooker so that you will not catch your sleeves or jewellery on them. This is especially important when younger brothers and sisters are around. They could easily knock a pan off and get burned or scalded.
- Always use an oven glove to take pans out of the oven. Don't use a wet cloth on a hot pan because the steam it produces could scald you.
- Lift the lid of a steaming pan with the opening away from you so that you will not get scalded.
- If you get burned or scalded, hold the burn in a bowl of cold water. Cold water helps to take the heat out of the burn. For more serious burns seek medical help immediately.
- If fat or cooking oil catches fire, throw bicarbonate of soda or salt at the bottom of the flame to put it out. (Water will not put out an oil or fat fire.) Call for help, and try to turn all the cooker controls to 'off'.

Cooking Utensils

colander – A bowl with holes in the bottom and sides. It is used for draining liquid from a solid food

skewer – A thin metal or wooden rod used to hold small pieces of food for grilling

slotted spoon – A spoon with small openings in its bowl. It is used to remove solid food from a liquid.

spatula – A flat, thin utensil, usually made from metal or wood, that is used to lift, toss, turn or scoop up food

tongs – A utensil shaped either like a pair of scissors or tweezers, with flat, blunt ends that are used to grasp food

Cooking Terms

brown – To cook food quickly over high heat so that the surface turns an even brown colour

garnish – To decorate with small pieces of food, such as parsley sprigs

sauté – To fry quickly over high heat in oil or fat, stirring or turning the food to prevent burning

simmer – To cook over a low heat in liquid kept just below its boiling point. Bubbles may occasionally rise to the surface.

stir-fry – To cook food in a small amount of oil over a high heat, stirring constantly.

Special Ingredients

allspice – A mildly scented spice prepared from the berries of the allspice tree

aubergine – A vegetable with shiny purple-black skin and cream-coloured flesh

black-eyed beans – Small, brown beans with a large black spot (from which they get their name)

chickpeas – Yellow in colour and slightly larger than green peas, chickpeas have a firm texture and a mild, nutty flavour

chilli – A small, hot, red or green pepper

cloves – Dried buds from a small evergreen tree. Cloves are used whole or ground to flavour food.

coconut milk – The white, milky liquid extracted from coconut flesh and used to give a coconut flavour to foods. It is available in tins at most supermarkets.

egusi seeds – Melon seeds with a pleasant nutty flavour. They can be bought at specialist shops.

garlic – A bulb-forming herb whose distinctive flavour is used in many dishes. Fresh garlic can usually be found in the fresh produce department of a supermarket. Each bulb can be broken up into sections called cloves. Most recipes only use a few cloves. Before you chop up a clove of garlic, you will have to remove the brittle, papery covering that surrounds it.

mango – A fruit grown in warm climates around the world. A mango has tough green skin that covers orange flesh and juice that is sweet and tart.

okra – Originating in Africa, okra are green vegetables with ridged skin and an oblong shape. Although they are sometimes available frozen or tinned, okra are best when fresh.

paprika – A dried and ground sweet red pepper, used for its flavour and its red colour

passatta – Prepared tomato sauce

peanut – A small, pale brown nut that can be eaten roasted or cooked or ground up in recipes.

plantain – A starchy fruit that looks like a banana and must be cooked before it is eaten

stock cubes – Small cubes that make stock when combined with hot water

thyme – A fragrant herb used fresh or dried to season food

tomato puree – Available in tins, jars or tubes, tomato puree is a richly flavoured concentrate. The tomatoes have been cooked for several hours, strained and the liquid has been taken out to create the deep red paste.

yams – A fleshy vegetable tuber popular in Africa, Asia, South America and the Caribbean. Yams contains natural sugar and have a texture that ranges from moist and tender to dry and coarse.

Healthy and Low-Fat Cooking Tips

Because West African cooking relies on many vegetables and legumes and not on cream and butter, many dishes are naturally low in fat. You can lower the fat content even further by eliminating the meat from the recipes. Some of the recipes for appetizers and desserts do require deep-frying. If you are particularly concerned about cutting fat from your diet, it's probably best not to make these recipes.

In general, there are many things you can do to prepare healthy, low-fat meals. Throughout the book, you'll find specific suggestions for individual recipes – don't worry, they'll still taste delicious! Here are a few general tips for adapting the recipes in this book.

Many recipes call for butter or oil to sauté vegetables or other ingredients. Using olive oil or canola oil instead of butter lowers saturated fat immediately, but you can also reduce the amount of oil you use – often by half. Sprinkling a little salt on the vegetables brings out their natural juices, so less oil is needed. It's also a good idea to use a small, non-stick frying pan if you decide to use less oil than the recipe calls for. Using cooking sprays to grease cooking dishes is an option, too.

Another common substitute for butter is margarine. Before making this substitution, consider the recipe. When desserts call for it, it's often best to use butter, as margarine may noticeably change the taste or consistency of the food.

You can lower the fat content of egg dishes by using an egg substitute in place of real eggs. When a recipe calls for tinned coconut milk, look for reduced-fat varieties. Many supermarkets stock 'light' coconut milk.

There are many ways to prepare meals that are good for you and still taste great. As you become a more experienced cook, try experimenting with recipes and substitutions to find the methods that work best for you.

This woman is selling fruit at a local market in Aného, Togo.

A West African Table

In West African villages, preparing dinner is a social event. Sisters and cousins go to the marketplace to buy fruit and fresh meat. Children pick fresh vegetables from the family garden. Making the meal may take up most of the day, but the cooks don't mind. This gives the women in the family a chance to talk and laugh. When the men return from a day's work, dinner is ready.

When serving a typical West African meal, cooks ladle the main dish of stew or soup onto individual plates. The starchy part of the meal, such as fufu, is served on a communal plate. The diners take turns using their right hands to scoop up small amounts of fufu. They roll the fufu into balls, then dip the balls into their stew and eat them. The starch of the fufu cools the heat of the main dish, which can be quite spicy.

Villagers in Senegal combine their efforts to pound grain. They are using pestles (large, thick sticks) and a mortar (large bowl) to do the job.

A West African Menu

West Africans traditionally eat two meals a day. The meals are basically the same. They are usually made up of a soup or stew served with some sort of starchy food, such as, fufu or rice. Below are two dinner menus with shopping lists of the items you'll need to prepare the meals. All the recipes can be found in this book.

DINNER 1

Vegetables in peanut sauce

Chickpea salad

Baked plantain on the shell

SHOPPING LIST:

Produce

2 onions
1 bulb of garlic
1.5 kg of tomatoes
2 green chilli peppers
2 carrots
1 white cabbage
150g of okra
1 red pepper
4 large, ripe plantains

Dairy/Egg/Meat

60g of butter

Tinned/Bottled/Boxed

vegetable oil
olive oil
50g of smooth unsalted
   peanut butter
500ml vegetable stock (fresh,
   or made with stock cubes)
800g of chickpeas
250g of mild or hot salsa

Other Ingredients

salt
pepper
thyme
allspice
brown sugar
cinnamon

DINNER 2

Fufu

Egusi soup

Fruit salad

Sweet balls

SHOPPING LIST:

Produce

4 to 6 large, ripe mangoes
4 medium bananas
3 large tomatoes
1 small onion
1 or 2 green chilli peppers
500g of fresh spinach
1.2kg sweet potatoes

Dairy/Egg/Meat

1-2 tbsp of margarine
1 egg
700g of beef tenderloin
900g of crab, shrimp or
    smoked fish

Tinned/Bottled/Boxed

vegetable oil
180g of instant mashed
    potato
160g of pineapple chunks
lime juice
peanut oil
200ml of passatta

Miscellaneous

salt
black pepper
sugar
375g desiccated coconut
425g of flour
130g of egusi or pumpkin
    seeds
baking powder
nutmeg

Staples and Snacks

Mildly flavoured staples such as fufu or rice are natural accompaniments to West Africa's hearty and spicy soups, stews and sauces. These foods are used as 'utensils' to scoop up other foods.

Although West Africans traditionally eat only two meals a day, one in the late morning and one in the evening, they eat snacks throughout the day. These snacks, which can also be served as appetizers, are usually very nutritious and actually amount to 'mini-meals'.

Ghanaians enjoy ntomo krako, *or sweet potato fritters (recipe on page 33), as a snack.*

Fufu

This is a Westernized version of fufu. To give your fufu a more authentic flavour, try leaving out the margarine and the salt.

water

1–2kg sweet potatoes (unpeeled)

1 tbsp of margarine (optional)

salt (optional)

pepper to taste

1. In a large saucepan, bring the water to the boil over a high heat. Reduce the heat to medium and add the sweet potatoes. Cook until soft, for about 35 minutes.

2. Drain the potatoes and allow to cool. Peel when cool.

3. Place in a bowl with the margarine and mash until soft. Season with salt and pepper.

4. Form the fufu into small balls and place on plates or in bowls.

Preparation time: 30 minutes
Serves 3-4

Sweet Potato Fritters / Ntomo Krako

Although the sweet potato isn't native to Africa, the root has made its way into many tasty West African recipes. This dish is popular in Ghana.

4 large sweet potatoes

1 tbsp of flour

1½ tbsp of peanut oil,* plus more for deep-frying

salt, to taste

2 tbsp of milk

2 eggs

dried bread crumbs

* Peanut oil is higher in saturated fat than some other oils. For a healthier alternative, you can use sunflower oil.

1. Wash and peel the potatoes. Cut them into chunks. Place the potatoes in a large saucepan and cover them with water. Bring the potatoes to the boil over a medium heat and cook them for 20 minutes, or until they can be easily pierced with a fork. Drain the water from the pan and let the potatoes cool.

2. Mash the potatoes. Slowly add the flour, 1½ tbsp of oil and the salt. Gradually add the milk. Stop mashing when the potatoes can be formed into small, smooth cakes. Form 1 tbsp of the mixture into 3-cm-thick fritters. Place the fritters on a plate until you are ready to cook them.

3. In a bowl, beat the eggs with a fork. Pour the bread crumbs into a saucer.

4. In a large saucepan or a deep-fat fryer, heat the oil for deep-frying to 190°C. Use a cooking thermometer to monitor the oil's heat. When the oil is ready, dip the sweet potato cakes into the egg and then cover them in bread crumbs. Fry the cakes for about 5 minutes, or until they are golden brown on both sides. Serve hot.

Preparation time: 50 minutes
Serves 4 to 6

Peanut Sauce

This sauce is made from peanuts. Peanut sauce is often substituted for meat dishes, although it is also served with dried meat and dried fish.

2 tbsp vegetable oil

I medium onion, peeled and chopped

2 medium tomatoes, cut into bite-sized pieces

I small aubergine, with or without peel, cut into bite-sized pieces

90g of smooth peanut butter*

60ml water

1. In a large frying pan, heat the oil over a medium heat for 1 minute. Add the onions and sauté until they become transparent.

2. Add the tomatoes and cook for 5 minutes. Add the aubergine and cook for 5 more minutes.

3. In a small bowl, combine the peanut butter and 60ml of water and stir to make a paste. Add this to the tomato-aubergine mixture and stir it well.

4. Reduce the heat to medium-low and simmer, uncovered, for 10 minutes, or until the aubergine is tender.

5. Serve with rice, potatoes, sweet potatoes or plantains.

Preparation time: 30 minutes
Serves 4 to 6

* This recipe works best if it is made with natural peanut butter that contains no added sugar.

Akara

This snack is often eaten with a sweet custard.

200g of dried black-eyed beans

80-120ml water

75g of onion, finely chopped

¼ tsp of black pepper

½ tsp of salt

½ tsp of chopped and deseeded
   chilli* or ¼ tsp of ground red
   chilli

1 egg

50-100g of finely chopped cooked
   prawns (optional)

vegetable oil

** Fresh chillies have to be handled
with care because they contain oils
that can burn your eyes and mouth.
After working with chillies, be sure
not to touch your face until you
have washed your hands thoroughly
with soap and water.*

1. Place the beans in a large, deep pan and cover them with water. Leave them to soak for a few hours or overnight.

2. With your hands under water in the pan, rub the beans together to remove the skins. The skins will float to the top and can be skimmed off. Drain the beans in a colander and place them into a blender or food processor with 80ml of water. Blend them for about 20 seconds or until they become smooth.

3. Place the ground beans into a bowl. If the mixture is dry, stir in water, little by little, until it is a paste.

4. Add the remaining ingredients except for the oil. Beat the mixture until it is light and airy. If, after adding the egg, the mixture is too runny, add 1 tbsp of flour.

5. In a large frying pan, heat a 2.5-cm depth of oil over a medium heat, until the temperature reaches 190°C. Use a cooking thermometer to monitor the oil's heat. Drop teaspoons of dough into the oil and fry for about 5 minutes or until they are golden brown. Remove the akara from the oil with a slotted spoon and drain them on pieces of kitchen towel. Serve immediately.

Preparation time: A few hours or overnight;

then 30 minutes

Serves 6

Peanut Balls / *Kulikuli*

Peanuts are grown in many parts of Africa. In northern Nigeria, the Hausa people use them to make kulikuli.

325g of shelled, roasted peanuts, unsalted

salt to taste

warm water

peanut oil

1. In a food processor or blender, grind the nuts until they are very fine.

2. Pour the peanuts onto a piece of kitchen towel to soak up any excess oil. Pour the nuts into a medium bowl.

3. Mix in the salt to taste and enough warm water to make a stiff dough.

4. Roll the peanut mixture into small balls and place them onto a clean plate.

5. In a large saucepan, heat 5-cm depth of peanut oil over a medium heat. Use a cooking thermometer to monitor the oil's heat. When it reaches 190°C, carefully place the balls into the oil.

6. Fry the balls for 5 minutes or until they turn golden brown.

7. Remove the balls with a slotted spoon and place them on pieces of kitchen towel to cool.

Preparation time: 25 minutes

Coconut Crisps

1 coconut*

* To open a coconut, bake it at 180°C
for 10 minutes. Remove the coconut
from the oven and hit it hard with
a hammer on the nut's seam. The
coconut will split open. Leave it
to cool before removing the flesh
from the shell.

1. Over a bowl, use a fork to remove the coconut flesh from the shell. Peel off the rind using a vegetable peeler. Cut the coconut into long, thin strips with a vegetable peeler.

2. Place the coconut onto a baking tray and grill it for 5 minutes or until it is lightly toasted. Watch the strips carefully, as they can burn quickly. Serve warm.

Preparation time: 25 minutes
Serves 6

Sweet Balls (Ghana)

1 egg

½ tsp of salt

3 tsp of baking powder

285g of sugar

½ tsp of nutmeg

350ml of warm water

375-425g of flour

vegetable oil

* Putting flour onto your
hands makes rolling the
dough much easier.

1. In a bowl, stir together the first five ingredients. Add the warm water and stir again. Gradually stir in enough flour so that the dough is slightly sticky.

2. Roll the dough* into balls the size of walnuts.

3. Pour 1.5-cm depth of oil into a deep pan and heat over a medium-high heat for 4 minutes. Fry the balls, a few at a time, for 3 to 4 minutes until they turn golden brown. Remove the balls and drain them on pieces of kitchen towel. Serve warm.

Preparation time: 45 minutes
Makes 25 to 30 balls

Fruit and Vegetables

Hundreds of varieties of fruit and vegetables grow in Africa, and they are an important part of West African cooking. What people don't grow in their own gardens, they buy at open-air markets that sell everything from bananas and cucumbers to guavas and yams. These fruit and vegetable dishes can be eaten alone as a snack, for a light lunch or supper, or they can be served as side dishes.

A colourful and nutritious fruit salad (recipe on page 42) can be made with a wide variety of locally grown fruits. Here, desiccated coconut is used as a garnish.

Fruit Salad

This salad is usually only served in wealthier households or for special occasions. Chunks of papaya can also be added.

4 to 6 large, ripe mangoes

4 medium bananas

1 large tomato (optional)

150g of pineapple chunks

juice from 1 medium lime

235ml of water

95g of sugar

40g of desiccated coconut
   to garnish

1. Wash and peel the mangoes and cut them into bite-sized cubes. Peel and slice the bananas. Cut the tomato in half, remove the seeds by squeezing each half over the sink and cut them into cubes.

2. Combine the mangoes, bananas, tomatoes and pineapple in a large bowl and mix, being careful not to mash the fruit.

3. In a small bowl, combine the lime juice, water and sugar. Stir well.

4. Pour the dressing over the fruit, cover and refrigerate for at least 1 hour. Mix well before serving. Garnish with the coconut.

Preparation time (including refrigeration):
1 hour and 20 minutes
Serves 4 to 6

Boiled Sweetcorn and Beans/ *Abrow ne Ase*

Sweetcorn is served all over Ghana.

600g of fresh sweetcorn, cut from the cob, or frozen sweetcorn

400g black-eyed beans, soaked (see page 36)

235ml of water

salt and freshly ground black pepper, to taste

1. Put the sweetcorn, the black-eyed beans and the water into a medium saucepan.

2. Cook, uncovered, over a medium heat for 5 minutes.

3. Sprinkle with salt and pepper to taste. Serve hot.

Preparation time: 10 to 30 minutes
Serves 6 to 8

Boiled Plantains

For variety, try adding tomatoes, onions, fresh spinach or a pinch of curry powder to boiled plantains.

2 large, firm green plantains

a pinch of salt

butter

1. Peel the plantains and cut them into 3-cm pieces. Place in a large pan.

2. Cover the plantains with water and add the salt.

3. Bring to the boil over a high heat. Reduce the heat to medium-low, cover and simmer for 10 minutes or until the plantains can be pierced with a fork. Serve hot with butter.

Preparation time: 15 minutes
Serves 4

Fried Plantains

3 large, ripe plantains

vegetable oil

1. Peel the plantains and slice them into thin circles.

2. In a large frying pan, heat 1cm depth of oil over a medium-high heat for 4 to 5 minutes. Fry the plantain slices for 4 to 5 minutes or until they turn golden brown on both sides.

3. Remove from the oil with a slotted spoon and drain them on pieces of kitchen towel.

Preparation time: 15 minutes
Serves 4

Grilled Plantains

2 or 3 large, ripe plantains

1. Cut the plantains in half lengthways and widthways. Do not peel.

2. Preheat the grill.

3. Grill the plantains, skin side down, for 5 to 7 minutes, or until they can be easily pierced with a fork and aren't sticky.

4. When they are cool enough to handle, peel the plantains and serve.

Preparation time: 15 minutes
Serves 4

Baked Plantain on the Shell

This recipe is an easy way to enjoy an exotic fruit.

4 large, ripe plantains

100g of brown sugar

¾ tsp of cinnamon

60g of butter or margarine, melted

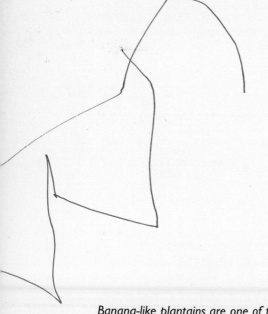

1. Preheat the oven to 180°C.

2. Wash the plantains and cut them in half lengthways. Do not peel.

3. Arrange them in a shallow, greased baking dish with their cut sides facing up.

4. In a small bowl, combine the brown sugar, cinnamon and melted butter. Stir well.

5. Pour the brown sugar mixture over the top of the plantains.

6. Cover the dish with aluminium foil and bake for 35 minutes or until the plantains are soft.

Preparation time: 45 minutes
Serves 4

Banana-like plantains are one of the most versatile fruits in West Africa. They can be boiled, fried, grilled or baked.

Soups

West African soups and sauces are quite similar to each other. Soups are served with a starchy food, such as fufu, on the side for dipping, while sauces, which are thicker than soups, are often served over a starchy food, such as rice.

When cooks prepare soups, they tend to make use of whatever fresh ingredients are available. Some soups contain meat, but meat-free soups are also popular and can be stretched to feed many people at once. West African cooks find many appetizing ways to combine vegetables and fish, with the zing of chillies or other distinctive spices.

Egusi soup (right, recipe on page 50) uses ground egusi seeds that give the dish a unique colour. If these are hard to find, the recipe works with pumpkin seeds. Fresh fish pepper soup (left, recipe on page 51) features hot chillies — a very characteristic flavouring in West African food.

Egusi Soup

130g of egusi or pumpkin seeds

700g of beef tenderloin*

¾ tsp of salt

¼ tsp of black pepper

60ml peanut oil

2 large tomatoes, chopped

1 small onion, peeled and chopped

1 or 2 green chilli peppers
    deseeded and chopped

200ml of passatta

350ml of water

any combination of fresh or tinned
    crab, fresh or tinned shrimp, or
    prawns or smoked fish adding up
    to 900g

450g of fresh spinach, cleaned and
    finely chopped

* To lower the fat content of this soup, use boneless, skinless chicken breasts instead of the beef.

1. Place the seeds into a blender or food processor and blend them for 30 to 40 seconds, until the seeds are a powdery paste. Empty into a bowl and set aside.

2. Wash the beef and cut it up into bite-sized cubes. Season it with salt and pepper.

3. In a large frying pan, heat the oil over a medium-high heat for 4 to 5 minutes. Add the beef and sauté for 3 to 5 minutes or until it is brown but not cooked through.

4. Place the tomatoes, onion and peppers in a clean blender or food processor. Blend for about 30 seconds, or until smooth.

5. Add the tomato mixture to the meat, reduce the heat to medium-low and cover. Cook for 1½ to 2 hours or until the meat is tender.

6. Add the passatta, water and seafood. Simmer for 10 minutes.

7. Add the spinach and ground seeds and continue to simmer for 10 more minutes. Serve with fufu.

Preparation time: 2 to 3 hours
Serves 6

Fresh Fish Pepper Soup

The combination of fish and chillies or hot peppers is very typical of West African cooking.

1kg of firm white filleted fish, cut into bite-sized pieces

1 litre of water

2 tomatoes

1 onion, peeled

3 to 4 sprigs of fresh parsley or 1 tsp of dried parsley

2 green chilli peppers, deseeded*

2 tsp of salt

1 tsp of dried thyme

1. Wash the fish, place it into a large saucepan and add the water.

2. Finely chop the tomatoes, onion, parsley and the chillies and add these to the water. Add the salt and thyme and stir.

3. Bring the mixture to the boil over a high heat. Reduce the heat to low, cover and simmer for 20 minutes.

4. Serve immediately.

Preparation time: 30 minutes
Serves 4 to 6

* By taking out the seeds, you will have sharp flavour but not fiery, hot taste.

Okra Soup

This recipe comes from Sierra Leone. To make this a vegetarian dish, leave out the meat and replace the beef stock with vegetable stock.

450g of stewing beef

1 tbsp of vegetable oil

1 large onion, thinly sliced

salt and freshly ground pepper,
    to taste

825ml of beef stock

8 small okra pods

2 small aubergines, sliced

3 tomatoes, peeled,* deseeded and
    coarsely chopped

To peel a tomato, place it in a small saucepan of boiling water for about 1 minute. Remove with a slotted spoon and leave it to cool until the tomato is warm but no longer hot. Use a small paring knife to peel off the skin. It should come off easily.

1. Cut the beef into small cubes. Heat the oil in a large pan and brown the beef.

2. Add the onion, the salt and the pepper and cook for 10 minutes, stirring occasionally.

3. Add the stock and bring the soup to the boil over a high heat.

4. Lower the heat and simmer, covered, for 30 minutes or until the beef is almost cooked.

5. In the meantime, wash the okra and cut the tops and bottoms off each pod.

6. Add the aubergine, tomatoes and okra. Simmer for another 15 minutes or until the vegetables are soft.

7. Remove the vegetables with a slotted spoon and put them into a blender. Blend until smooth.

8. Return the blended vegetables to the pot, adjust the seasonings and cook for 5 more minutes. Serve hot.

Preparation time: 1 hour and 30 minutes
Serves 4

Main Dishes

In West Africa, families tend to eat their main meal in the evening. Cooks often have to cope with having only a few ingredients, but they have become skilled at substituting and at stretching a little food a long way. By combining vegetables, meat and a starchy food into one-pot meals, cooks can feed many people. On special occasions, however, the dishes may be served separately.

The ingredients of jollof rice (recipe on page 56) – lots of different vegetables, rice and sometimes meat – make it filling, nutritious and colourful.

Jollof Rice

Jollof rice is a well-known West African dish. It can be made with chicken, beef or no meat at all.

4 to 6 pieces of skinless chicken

½ tsp of salt

½ tsp of black pepper

60ml of vegetable oil

1 medium onion, peeled and finely chopped

115g of cubed ham

2 chicken stock cubes

¼ tsp of ground chilli

½ tsp of dried thyme or 1 sprig fresh thyme, crushed

350ml of water

170g of tomato puree

260g of uncooked rice

any combination of green peas, chopped French beans, carrots, green peppers or tomatoes, adding up to 300g

1. Season the chicken with salt and black pepper. In a large frying pan, heat the oil over a medium-high heat for 3 to 4 minutes. Add the chicken pieces and brown them on both sides.

2. Place the chicken into a large saucepan and set it aside. Add the ham and onion to the frying pan and sauté until the onion is transparent. Add both the onion and the ham to the saucepan and set the frying pan aside. (Do not discard the oil.)

3. Add the stock cubes, red pepper, thyme, water and tomato puree to the saucepan and stir well. Simmer over a low heat for about 10 minutes.

4. Add the rice to the frying pan and stir to coat it with the oil. Add the rice and vegetables to the saucepan, stir well and cover. Cook over a low heat for 35 to 40 minutes, or until the vegetables and rice are tender.

Preparation time: 1 hour and 30 minutes
Serves 4 to 6

Spinach Stew

This is a very quick meal for city dwellers in West Africa, who have easy access to convenient tinned and frozen foods. Spinach stew takes little time to prepare and is very nutritious.

175ml of vegetable oil

1 small onion, peeled and cubed

1 small tomato, cubed

85g of tomato puree

450g of fresh spinach, cleaned and chopped

350g of corned beef*

1 tsp of ground chilli

1 tsp of salt

4 to 6 servings of cooked rice

1. In a large frying pan, heat the oil over a medium heat for 1 minute. Add the onion and sauté until it is transparent (for about 5 minutes).

2. Add the tomato and tomato puree and cook for 5 minutes. Add the remaining ingredients except for the rice, cover and cook for 30 to 35 minutes over a medium-high heat.

3. Serve over the rice.

Preparation time: 1 hour
Serves 4 to 6

* To make this a vegetarian dish, you can leave out the corned beef.

Vegetables in Peanut Sauce

I tbsp of vegetable oil

150g of onion, chopped

3 cloves of garlic

45g of unsalted smooth peanut
    butter

1.5 kg of tomatoes peeled,
    deseeded and pureed
    (or use tinned)

500ml of vegetable stock

800ml of water

I tsp of thyme

2 green chilli peppers, chopped

¼ tsp of allspice

I tsp of salt

2 carrots, peeled and sliced

700g of shredded white cabbage*

250g of fresh okra, sliced into
    3-cm pieces

I red pepper, chopped

*Try using a serrated knife
to slice the cabbage rather
than shredding it.*

1. Heat the oil in a large, heavy frying pan and sauté the onion and garlic for 3 minutes. Stir to prevent it from burning. Mix in the peanut butter and the tomatoes and simmer for 1 minute.

2. In a saucepan, bring the vegetable stock to the boil. Lower the heat to a simmer and cook until only half of the stock remains.

3. In a separate saucepan, combine the water, thyme, chillies, allspice, salt and 80ml of the reduced vegetable stock. Bring the mixture to the boil. Turn the heat down to a simmer and cook for 30 minutes, uncovered. Stir occasionally. The consistency should be slightly thick.

4. Pour the remaining stock into a medium saucepan and bring it to the boil. Add the carrots, cabbage, okra and pepper. Reduce the heat to low and simmer. Cook for about 15 minutes or until the vegetables are just starting to get tender.

5. Drain the vegetables and put them into a warm serving dish. Pour the peanut sauce over the vegetables and serve.

Preparation time: 1 hour and 15 minutes
Serves 4

Casamance Fish Stew / *Kaldou*

Serve this stew, which originated in the Casamance region of Senegal, over rice.

1kg of skinless, filleted red snapper or cod,

120ml of lemon juice

2 tbsp of peanut oil

2 large onions, sliced

950ml of water

1 red chilli pepper, pricked with a fork

1. Wash the fish in cold water and pat it dry with pieces of kitchen towel.

2. Rub 1 tbsp of the lemon juice onto the fish.

3. In a big frying pan, heat the oil.

4. Cook the onion slices in the oil until they are soft and golden.

5. Add the water and the chilli pepper to the pan.

6. Bring the mixture to the boil and add the fish.

7. Reduce the heat and cook, uncovered, for 10 minutes.

8. Add the rest of the lemon juice and cook for 3 more minutes.

9. Take out the chilli and serve hot with rice.

Preparation time: 30 minutes
Serves 4

Curry

1kg of chicken, lamb or beef, cut up into bite-sized pieces

1 slice of lime or lemon

salt to taste

1 clove of garlic, crushed

235ml of water

60-120ml of peanut oil

2 onions, chopped

½ to 1 tbsp of cayenne pepper

6 tomatoes, peeled and sliced

1 tbsp of curry powder

tomato sauce

1 small potato, peeled and diced

½ tsp of thyme

275g of okra, sliced (you can use fresh or frozen okra in this recipe).

175ml of evaporated milk*

250g of rice, cooked

1. Wash the meat in cold water and pat it dry with pieces of kitchen towel.

2. Rub the meat with the slice of lime or lemon.

3. Place the meat onto a plate and sprinkle it with the salt and the garlic. Leave it to stand for 1 hour.

4. In a large pot, simmer the meat in the water until it is tender.

5. Remove the meat and place it onto a clean plate. Don't discard the stock.

6. Heat the oil in a frying pan and brown the meat.

7. Add the onions, cayenne pepper, tomatoes, curry powder, tomato sauce, potato, thyme and stock.

8. Cook on a low heat until the meat is tender and the vegetables are almost cooked.

9. Add the okra and cook until they are soft.

10. Add the evaporated milk and heat to serving temperature.

11. Serve over rice.

* To lower the fat content of this dish, use low-fat evaporated milk.

*Preparation time: 1 hour and 30 minutes
(plus 1 hour to marinate)
Serves 4*

Festival Food

No matter what the occasion – and there are many of them – West Africans associate good times with a wide variety of delicious foods. In fact, the harvesting of some foods is the occasion for celebration. *Futari* (recipe on page 68), for example, is a favourite dish during the Iri-Ji, or yam, festival in Nigeria. Freshwater fish are the focus of the Argungu festival.

Because some ingredients are costly, cooks tend to wait until a festival to prepare some of the more elaborate dishes. Chicken is particularly hard to find. Separating the starchy foods, meat and vegetables from one another – rather than combining them into one dish – also tends to be more common during festivals.

Chicken yassa (recipe on pages 64 and 65) is cooked on special occasions in Senegal. The long marination and the use of red chilli peppers and their seeds make this a spicy, hot dish.

Chicken Yassa / *Yassa au Poulet*

This dish is served at special occasions in Senegal.

60ml of lemon juice

4 large onions, sliced

salt and freshly ground black
    pepper, to taste

5 tbsp of peanut oil

1 red chilli pepper

1-2kg of chicken pieces

120ml of water

1. Prepare the marinade the night before you plan to cook this dish. In a deep bowl, mix the lemon juice, onions, salt, pepper and 4 tbsp of peanut oil.

2. Use a fork to prick holes in the chilli pepper and add it to the marinade whole.

3. Leave the marinade to stand for 15 minutes and then check the spiciness of the sauce. If it is hot enough for your taste, remove the pepper. If not, let the mixture stand for a bit longer.

4. Add the chicken to the marinade and stir to coat it thoroughly.

5. Cover the bowl with cling film and store it in the fridge overnight.

6. To cook the next day, preheat the grill.

7. Remove the chicken pieces from the marinade and place them on a piece of aluminium foil on the grill rack.

8. Grill the pieces briefly, until they are lightly browned on both sides.

9. Remove from the grill, place on a plate and set aside.

10. Strain the onions from the marinade by pouring the mixture through a sieve held over a bowl.

11. In a large frying pan, heat 1 tbsp of oil over medium heat.

12. Add the onions and sauté them until they are soft and tender.

13. Add the rest of the marinade and cook until the mixture is heated through evenly.

14. Add the browned chicken pieces and water to the pan. Stir to coat.

15. Lower the heat, bring the contents of the pan to a simmer and cover. Cook for at least 30 minutes or until the chicken pieces are completely cooked. Serve the yassa hot over rice.

Marinating time: overnight
Cooking time: 45 minutes
Serves 6

Ginger-Fried Fish

1 kg of firm white fish fillets, such as haddock, cod or halibut

½ tbsp of ground ginger

1 onion, finely chopped

½ tsp of cayenne pepper

salt to taste

2 tbsp of peanut or corn oil

sprigs of parsley

1. Wash the fish under cold water and pat it dry with pieces of kitchen towel. Remove the skin.

2. Cut the fish into small 2.5-cm pieces and place them in a medium bowl.

3. Add the ground ginger, onion, cayenne pepper and salt. Stir to combine and leave to stand for 15 minutes.

4. Heat the oil in a frying pan over a medium-high heat. Add the fish to the oil and use a spatula to turn it, allowing the fillets to fry on all sides.

5. Serve the fish hot over rice. Garnish with the sprigs of parsley.

Preparation time: 40 minutes
Serves 4

Ginger-fried fish might be served at the celebrations following the Yoruba naming ceremony. The Yoruba are one of the main ethnic groups in Nigeria.

Yams and Squash / *Futari*

Futari is a popular dish at the Nigerian Iri-Ji festival.

2 tbsp of vegetable oil

1 onion, finely chopped

450g of squash, skinned*
    and cut into 2.5-cm pieces
    (discard the seeds)

2 yams or sweet potatoes, peeled*
    and cut into 2.5-cm pieces

235ml of coconut milk

½ tsp of salt

½ tsp of ground cinnamon

¼ tsp of ground cloves

1. Heat the oil in a Dutch oven or a large saucepan over a medium-high heat.

2. Add the onion and fry it for about 3 minutes, until it becomes soft. Stir constantly.

3. Add the squash, yams or sweet potatoes, coconut milk, salt, cinnamon and cloves. Stir to combine.

4. Bring the mixture to the boil and then reduce the heat to bring it to a simmer. Cover and cook for 10 minutes.

5. Uncover and cook for 5 more minutes, or until the vegetables are tender, stirring occasionally. Serve hot in bowls.

Preparation time: 30 minutes
Serves 6 to 8

* Use a potato peeler to peel the squash and the sweet potatoes.

Chickpea Salad

This salad is a welcome addition to the lamb served at Eid ul-Fitr celebrations in West Africa.

600g of tinned chickpeas, including the liquid

1 tbsp of olive oil

1 onion, finely chopped

150g of mild or hot salsa

salt and pepper, to taste

1. Pour the chickpeas, with the liquid, into a medium bowl.

2. Add the olive oil, onion, salsa and salt and pepper to taste.

3. Stir to combine. Refrigerate until ready to serve.

Preparation time: 10 minutes
Serves: 6

Peanut Cookies

In Burkina Faso, Christians make these tasty biscuits during the Christmas season.

500g of finely chopped, salted peanuts

3 eggs

200g brown sugar, firmly packed

3 tbsp of flour

¼ tsp of baking powder

1. Preheat the oven to 180°C.

2. In a medium bowl, combine the peanuts, eggs, brown sugar, flour and baking powder. Use a spoon or mixer to stir the ingredients until they are well blended.

3. Place tablespoonfuls of the dough 2.5 cm apart on a baking tray.

4. Bake for 10 minutes or until the cookies are lightly browned.

Preparation time: 45 minutes
Makes 3 dozen cookies

Index

About the Authors

Bertha Vining Montgomery grew up in Social Circle, Georgia, USA. She graduated from Spelman College in Georgia with a degree in home economics. Montgomery has taught in all areas of home economics at high school level. She would like to thank Janet Clemetson, Farha Ibrahim, the Lawal family, Rukiya Mahmood and Uche Iheagwara for their help and encouragement with this book.

Constance Nabwire was born and raised in Uganda. She attended King's College Budo in Uganda before going to the USA on the African Student Programme for American Universities. After earning a degree in sociology and psychology from Spelman College in Georgia, Nabwire attended the University of Minnesota on a fellowship by the American Association of University Women and graduated with a masters degree in social work. Nabwire has also published several short stories and articles about her native land. Nabwire would like to thank her friends, who contributed their ideas and recipes to this book.

Photo Acknowledgements

The photographs in this book are reproduced courtesy of: © Pius Utomi Ekpei/AfP/ Getty Images, pp 2-3; © istockphoto.com/Ines Gesell, p 25; © Louiseann and Walter Pietrowicz/September 8th Stock, pp 4 (left), 5 (right), 18, 30, 37, 47, 53, 59, 62, 67; © Robert L & Diane Wolfe, pp 4 (right), 5 (left), 6, 34, 40, 44, 48, 54; © Victor Englebert, p 10; © Paul Almasy/CORBIS, p 11; Dr Deborah Pellow, p 13; © Marcus Rose/Panos Pictures, pp 14-15; Yosef Hadar/WORLD BANK PHOTO, p 17; Hans-Olaf Pfannkuch, p 26.

Cover photos (front, back and spine): © Louiseann and Walter Pietrowicz/ September 8th Stock.

The illustrations on pages 7, 19, 27, 31, 33, 35, 36, 39, 41, 49, 50, 51, 52, 55, 57, 58, 61, 63, 65 and 68 and the map on page 8 are by Tim Seeley/Independent Picture Service.

First published in the United States of America in 2002